15/Aug/90

HISTORICAL ZANZIBAR

ROMANCE OF THE AGES

Introduction and captions by Professor Abdul Sheriff
Photographs from Zanzibar Archives

HISTORICAL ZANZIBAR

ROMANCE OF THE AGES

Published by HSP Publications
First edition 1995

CONTENTS

HISTORICAL ZANZIBAR

Previous page: Foradhani sea front before 1896.
Top left going clock-wise: Seyyid Humoud bin Muhammad, Ruler of Zanzibar (1896-1902); The old navigator's tower which formerly stood in front of Beit al-Ajaib; Kufic inscription in Kizimkazi mosque built in 1107 AD; An ivory market; Lloyd Mathews and officials together with prominent citizens and the Sultan's soldiers.

HISTORICAL ZANZIBAR

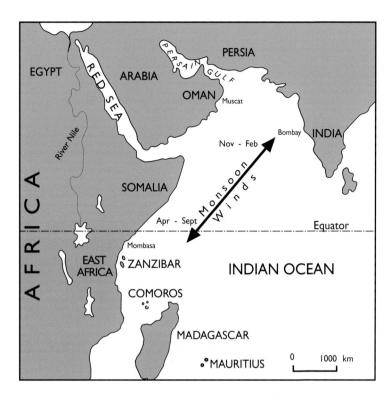

Zanzibar: between Africa and the Indian Ocean. The monsoon winds connected Zanzibar with the Orient, which was important for its trade and its history.

ROMANCE OF THE AGES

Zanzibar! The very name conjures up the romance of the ages. For a small country, Zanzibar occupies a very large space in the world's imagination. It was a place where Africa met the Orient across the Indian Ocean, an arena of commerce and cultural interaction.

From at least the beginning of the Christian era Arab merchants have been intermingling with the people on the coast of Azania, from which the name Zanzibar is said to take its root. Zanguebar, the land of the Zanj (blacks), was one of the marvels of the East. The fantasies about a far-off island paradise, where myths of elephants' tusks and aromatic spices, oriental princesses and African slaves were strangely intertwined, were the stuff on which stories of Sindbad the Sailor were based. According to the Italian traveler Marco Polo, it was populated by a nation of giants and equally gigantic *rukh* birds who could pick up whole elephants. Not only the name but also the many marvellous stories of the medieval era associated with it were inherited by this small island off the East African coast.

To this heritage Zanzibar has added its own romance from it reached its prime in the nineteenth century. It was then the capital of an Afro-Arab dynasty, a centre of international diplomacy and commerce, a seat of learning and itinerant *ulema* (Muslim religious scholars), and a gateway to Africa. Through its portals passed not only slaves, spices and ivory, but also missionaries, explorers and conquerors. Harems, palace intrigues and the elopement of a Zanzibari princess to Europe refurbished the romantic image of Zanzibar.

ZANZIBAR IN ITS PRIME

This romance was rudely interrupted by the reality of European expansionism in the sixteenth century. The Portuguese crusaders, in the name of Christianity and commerce, had introduced military force, which had previously been relatively insignificant in the commercial world of the Indian Ocean.

After the expulsion of the Portuguese from the East African coast at the end of the seventeenth century by the Swahili and their Omani allies, the latter gradually extended their hegemony over the East African coast. During the nineteenth century Zanzibar became so prosperous that the Busaidi ruler of Oman, Seyyid Said bin Sultan (1804-1856), transferred his capital from Muscat in Oman to the erstwhile colony of Zanzibar in around 1840.

Seyyid Said built his first palace at Mtoni, a few miles north of the town where he continued to spend part of the week. Later he built his town palace, Beit al-Sahel, the Palace by the Sea, where he held his court. It was attended by Omani landowners and other dignitaries, dressed in their fine robes and turbans. There they exchanged greetings and sipped coffee while engaging in informal consultation with their sovereign.

Seyyid Said, who descibed himself as 'only a merchant', realised the economic potential of Zanzibar. The price of spices from the East was still exorbitantly high as a result of the Dutch monopoly over the trade, so he encouraged the expansion of the clove plantations on Zanzibar. The islands were to emerge as the most important producer of the spice in the world, yielding nearly four-fifths of the world's supply of cloves until the middle of the twentieth century. So profitable was the enterprise that the *'clove mania'* encroached heavily on the islands' second major crop, coconut, which was used by Zanzibaris for cooking as well as for export. [16-18]

These plantations were established when slaves were still the normal source of plantation labour. In the British colonies slavery was not abolished until the 1830s; in the United States of America not until the 1860s. In Zanzibar it was abolished in 1897, and in the British and German colonies of East Africa even later. As a result there was an enormous expansion in the slave trade from the interior of Africa. A small number were exported to the north, and some slave *dhows* were intercepted by British warships after all the external slave trade was made illegal in 1845. However, a much larger number were absorbed by the plantations on the islands and on the East African coast. Many were also used in the households as domestics and in the towns to provide social services, such as sanitation. [22, 23, 26]

The other sector of the economy was commerce, and Zanzibar developed as a major entrepôt for the whole of eastern Africa. The Sultan was a shrewd merchant prince. With the peace after the end of the Napoleonic wars, he sought to expand the Omani role in the commerce of the Indian Ocean. He built on his good relations with the British by encouraging trade with British India and offering protection to the ubiquitous Indian traders and financiers in Muscat and Zanzibar. To expand trade with the West he signed a number of commercial treaties with the United States of America (1833), Great Britain (1839) and France (1844), which were to be followed under his successors by the Hanseatic Republics of Northern Germany (1859) and other European states.

Zanzibar was then a cosmopolitan metropole. Its harbour teemed with oriental *dhows* with their lateen sails and the square-rigged vessels from the West, carrying all the colours of the rainbow. Here Yankee merchants from New England sold their *Marekani* cloth to Indian traders in return for ivory. The French from Marseilles haggled with the Somali for hides and sesame seeds. And the entrepreneurs from Hamburg shipped hundreds of tons of cowrie shells to West Africa where they served as currency [8].

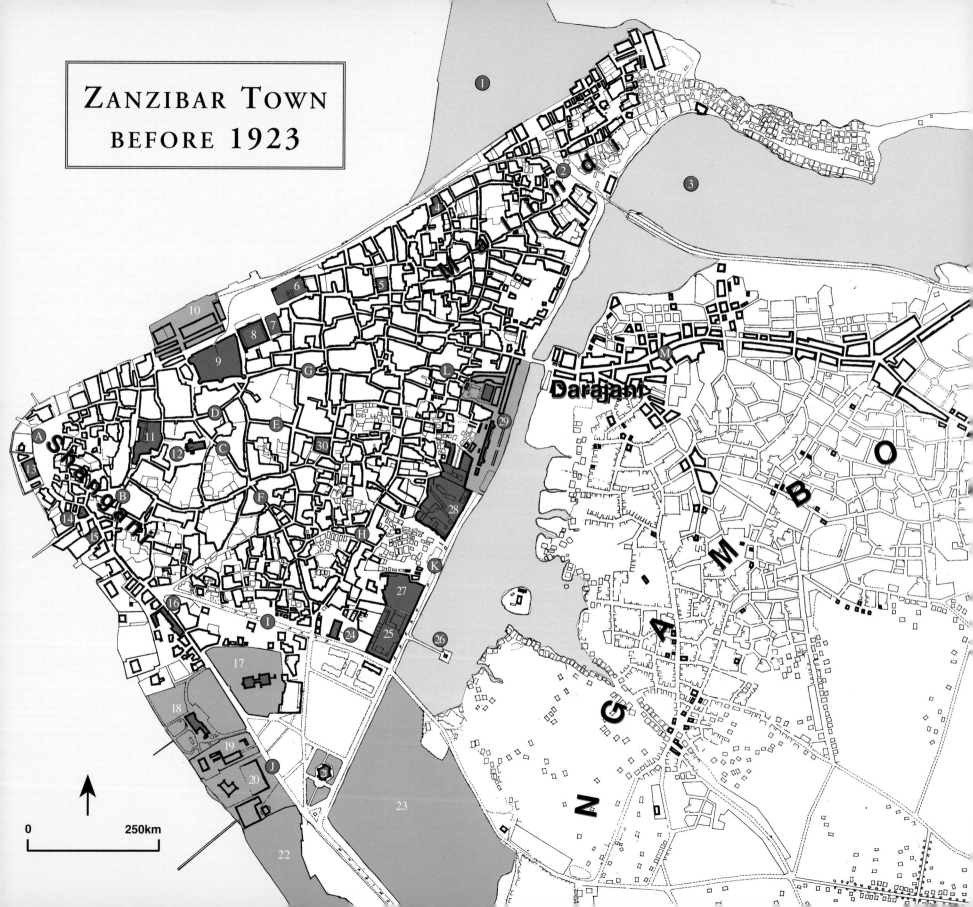

KEY TO MAP

Landmarks and Important Buildings

1   Site of reclaimed harbour [74]
2   Railway passing through Malindi [70]
3   Creek which is now reclaimed land [28, 34]
4   Khoja Hospital (Ithna' sheri Dispensary) [75]
5   French Consulate
6   Once the site of Sultans' Palace [38, 44, 45]
7   Once the site of Beit al-Hukm [38]
8   Beit al-Ajaib (House of Wonders) [8, 39, 48}
9   Old Fort (Railway Workshops in 1920's)
10 Customs (now Jamhuri Gardens)
11 Post Office [55]
12 Roman Catholic Church [33]
13 Eastern Telegraphic Company Building (now Serena Hotel)
14 Tippu Tip House
15 English Club (Africa House Hotel)
16 Her Britannic Majesty's Court (Courts of Law) [65]
17 Victoria Garden [78]
18 British Residency (now State House) [52]
19 Native Hospital
20 European Hospital
21 Peace Memorial Museum
22 Cemetery
23 Mnazimoja Recreation Ground
24 Majestic Cinema
25 Former Government Stables
26 Wireless Station
27 Public Works Department store
28 English Mission (site of the old slave market) [34, 35]
29 Markets
30 Hamamni Baths

Main Streets

A   Shangani Street
B   Main Street (now Kenyatta Road) [54, 55]
C   Cathedral Street
D   Portuguese Street (now Gizenga Street)
E   Hamamni Street
F   Soko Ya Mhogo Street
G   Hurumzi Street
H   Mkunazini Street
I   Vuga Road
J   Mnazimoja Road
K   Creek Road
L   Kiponda Street
M   Darajani Street (leading to the plantations)

Symbol Key

Substantial buildings   **Bold Lines**
Important buildings
Important area
Reclaimed land
Indian Ocean
[Numbers in square brackets refer to plate numbers]

On the other hand, Zanzibar's hinterland extended deep into the interior of Africa. Trading parties organised by Africans from the interior brought ivory and other commodities to the coast where they exchanged them for cloth, metal wires and beads. Simultaneously, caravans like those of Tippu Tip, financed by Indian merchants, penetrated beyond the Great Lakes and the Mountains of the Moon into eastern Zaire, and some even reached the Atlantic coast in Angola. [30, 61]

In that age of African exploration such an economic and diplomatic centre naturally recommended itself to missionaries and explorers as a place from where to fit out their expeditions into the African interior. The German missionary Ludwig Krapf sought the protection of Seyyid Said for his missionary activities on the African mainland. It was also a place where all the famous explorers, including Richard Burton and David Livingstone, began their journeys. Henry Morton Stanley, the American journalist who was sent to find Livingstone, also used Zanzibar as a base, where he met Zanzibari dignitaries at a colourful function. [32]

Befitting such a cosmopolitan centre, religious tolerance was a byword. Although the ruling dynasty belonged to the small puritanical Ibadhi muslim sect, the majority Sunni as well as a number of Shia sects enjoyed complete freedom to practice their religion. That toleration extended equally to the Hindus who built their temples, as well as to the Christians. The devout but tolerant Muslim Sultan, Seyyid Said, wrote in his letter of introduction to his governors that the Christian missionary Ludwig Krapf was 'a good man who wishes to convert the world to God. Behave well to him and be everywhere serviceable to him'. The Anglicans built their cathedral on the site of the former slave market, while the Roman Catholics built theirs, designed by the famous architect of the basilica of Marseilles, off Gizenga Street. [33-35]

Rebellion & the Elopement of a Princess

The history of Zanzibar in the nineteenth century was by no means one of perfect tranquillity. One source of turbulence was the extremely personal nature of the political system in which succession depended on "the length of one's sword". When Sayyid Said died in 1856 the British supported the division of his kingdom into the Omani and Zanzibari halves between his two eldest sons. The fiery third son, Seyyid Barghash, immediately raised the standard of rebellion which was suppressed with the intervention of the British marines. This was the first intervention that was ultimately to lead to the subjugation of the sultanate to the British during the Partition for Africa.

Among Seyyid Barghash's supporters who played an active role in the rebellion was one of his half-sisters, Seyyida Salme. Born of a Circassian concubine, she had grown up at the Mtoni

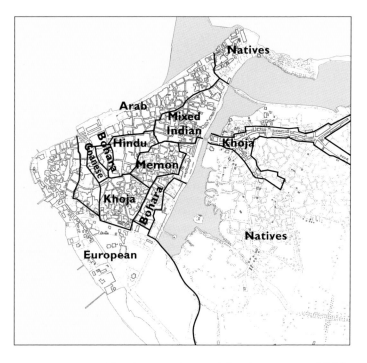

Map showing the racial distribution around 1923

Palace before moving to the town. There, across the narrow street she formed a liaison with a German trader with whom she eloped to Germany in 1866. In her later years she wrote her autobiography, the first by a Zanzibari, and also the first by any Muslim woman, giving a marvellous account of the life of a princess in Zanzibar.

The suppression of the rebellion left the British in a dominant position in Zanzibar. Although Seyyid Barghash tried to re-establish his autonomy when he became Sultan in 1870, he was forced to witness the dismantling of his father's commercial empire. He was only spared the imposition of British colonial rule over Zanzibar itself in 1890, two years after his death. Thereafter, the British very much chose whoever was most pliant to place on the throne.

But the spirit of Seyyid Barghash was not yet dead, although the reality had changed completely. In 1896 his son Khalid claimed the throne to re-establish the autonomy of Zanzibar. In a clear demonstration of the impotence of the Arab sultanate in the face of the new imperial power, the British issued an ultimatum at the end of which they bombarded the Palace. In what is described as "the shortest war in history", the Palace was in ruins within 45 minutes. Khalid sought refuge in the German consulate, and later in German East Africa. He was never to set foot in Zanzibar again. [40-47]

Modern Zanzibar

Modern Zanzibar began to take its shape during the long reign of Seyyid Khalifa bin Haroub (1911-1960). The Sultan retained the dignity and façade of an Arab state, and Arab grandees were accorded respect and were often consulted in matters of state. But control of the administration was firmly in the hands of the colonial governor, the British Resident. There was a modern army under European officers, and Her Britannic Majesty's Court, with Arab and Indian interpreters, was set up to administer justice. An administrative bureaucracy, employing a number of Parsi and other civil servants, attended to the day-to-day business of government. In due course participation by the leaders of the local communities in the affairs of state was formalised by the establishment of the Protectorate Council, and later the Legislative Council, which included a minority of appointed Arab and Indian, and ultimately African, leaders. [65]

Zanzibar also began to have the paraphernalia of a modern state. Seyyid Barghash, who had spent his years of exile in Bombay in the 1860s, and had visited England in 1872, was impressed by the modern amenities that he saw there. He constructed a seven-mile-long aqueduct to bring fresh stream water to the town, and he introduced electricity to the area around the Palace, apparently the first town in sub-Saharan Africa to have electricity.

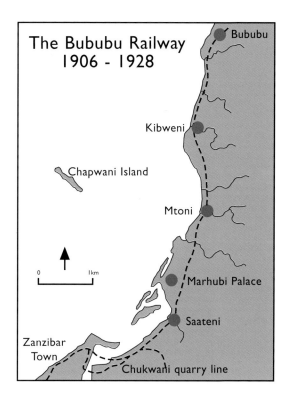

The Bububu Railway
1906 - 1928

Bububu

Kibweni

Chapwani Island

Mtoni

Marhubi Palace

Saateni

Zanzibar
Town

Chukwani quarry line

Zanzibar also had a seven-mile railway from the town to Bububu at the edge of the clove plantation area. It was built by an American company and carried passengers and produce to the town
market. In the early part of the twentieth century Zanzibar began to see other forms of transport,
such as the motor car beginning to take the place of horse-drawn carriages, including a horse-drawn
ambulance. In the face of competition from motor buses, the railway was not extended as was
planned, and it was eventually uprooted in 1928. [69-73]

No state would be complete without a prison. In the nineteenth century the Old Fort was used as
a jail. After the establishment of colonial rule the British began to build a prison on Prison Island,
which lay opposite the harbour, but the plans were later abandoned. Instead, a town jail was built
a mile to the south of the town; it is still in use. [67]

In the nineteenth century the peninsula on which the town is situated provided shelter to the *dhows*
and other vessels at anchor, and goods could be landed directly on shore. With the growth in the
size of the ships a need was identified for a deep water harbour. In the 1920s a new wharf was built
at Malindi. Stones were quarried at Chukwani, seven miles to the south of the town, and transported by a light railway. [71, 72, 74]

The Old Stone Town

The Old Town of Zanzibar has encapsulated within it the essence of its nineteenth-century great-
ness, though now much decayed. It consisted of palaces and *hamams*, of beautifully carved doors
on the massive but simple mansions of the landowners, of winding bazaars and a babble of lan-
guages. The sea front is dominated by the Old Fort and the palaces of the Sultans, which reached
a new height of flamboyance in the age of Seyyid Barghash (1870-1888). Apart from refurbishing
the old palaces, he built the imposing Beit al Ajaib (House of Wonders) for state ceremonial func-
tions. He also built a number of country palaces, such as that at Marhubi which was destroyed by
a fire at the end of the nineteenth century The House of Wonders, damaged during the bombardment of 1896, was repaired. A new tower was added to the roof in place of the old tower which had
formerly stood in front of it. [1, 2, 8, 38, 48, 49]

The Palace complex was flanked by the massive but simple mansions of the Omani landowners
with small, square external windows. They were marked only by their elaborately carved wooden
doors, exhibiting modest riches and subdued elegance typical of the puritanical Ibadhis. But the
simple façade hid much that was richer in the arches around the inner courtyard and niches in the
carpeted and decorated rooms. They were occupied by prosperous landowners and merchants who
attended the Sultan's court, that is, when they were not engaged in disposing their crops of cloves,

or negotiating a mortgage for their plantations.

The sea front mansions hid a labyrinth of bazaars where the merchants lived. Originally built on a more modest scale with a narrow shop fronting the bazaar and residential quarters above, some of the Indian merchants' houses later developed into elaborate *havelis* with intricate wooden verandahs to catch the breeze, and distinctive carved doors.

The town was not as segregated in the nineteenth century as it became during the colonial period when the Old Creek divided it sharply between the Stone Town and Ngambo on the other side. Huts inhabited by the poorer sections of the population, including slaves and the emancipated and free workers, were interspersed all over the town. [18, 19]

A Cosmopolitan Metropole

Zanzibar is indeed a living museum. With an area of only about a thousand square miles and a history that stretches back more than a thousand years, every person in its cosmopolitan population, and every house in the Old Stone Town, has a story to tell about its complex and intriguing history. It is located at the confluence of the world of continental Africa and the maritime world of the Indian Ocean. It has a history of invasions, and of assimilation of the invaders in the integrated culture of Zanzibar. It is a cultural mosaic that has a pattern and a meaning that would be lost if the pieces were separated and identified individually as African, Arab, Indian, etc. It can only be identified as Zanzibari.

Zanzibar is a lode that still attracts visitors from all over the world, and it continues to tug at the hearts of the nostalgic Zanzibari exiles, dispersed by the revolutionary winds. It has an irresistible attraction for tourists and scholars, as it did during the days of the monsoon *dhows*. They can come as the Arab travellers Masudi and Ibn Battuta did so many centuries ago, eager to see and learn about a unique civilisation; or they can come as Vasco da Gama and Karl Peters, to conquer and dominate. They can help develop a vibrant but fragile culture, or they can try to deface it. Comparing the photographs of Historical Zanzibar in this volume with the living reality, however, one cannot escape the conclusion that the small island has shown remarkable resilience. It has changed with each encounter, but it has nevertheless survived foreign invasions and internal revolutions; it has invariably absorbed the settlers and the invaders, and made them its own.

The reality may not correspond to the fantasy some people may have about Zanzibar, but few leave it disappointed.

ZANZIBAR
AT ITS PRIME

Sultan's Palace with boat made of stone which
served as a water container. Before 1890.

2 Sea front of the Stone Town before the harbour was built.

3 View of the Stone Town from the top of Beit al-Ajaib.

4

A narrow street in the Old Stone Town of Zanzibar.

5
An old mosque.

6

Chukwani Palace, built by Sultan Barghash (1870-88), the great monument builder of Zanzibar in 1872. Primarily used as a place to recover after illness as the air here was supposed to be healthy, eight miles south of the town. Most of the original building has been demolished.

7

Marhubi Palace, also built by Sultan Barghash, was one of his country palaces, three miles north of the town. Built with coral and wood it was destroyed by fire in 1899.

8

The sea front of Zanzibar, showing the Beit al-Ajaib (House of Wonders). On the left were *godowns* of the port with *dhows* anchored in front before the new harbour was built in the 1920s. In the centre is an outrigger *ngalawa* with unusual European-type sails instead of the normal lateen sail.

9

A Zanzibari, wearing a *tarboush* cap, proudly posing with his bicycle in a studio.

10

Omani Arab women in complete *purdah* (veil). Normally they wore a *barakoa* which covered their faces but left open the eyes.

12

Masingini Ridge, the highest point in Zanzibar. Man-made beauty in Zanzibar is complemented by natural beauty. The 'Pink Terraces' are a handsome collection of earth pillars formed by water erosion.

11

An inside view of the Palace residential quarters, with a young prince in the centre. Note the muskets hanging down on the wall, typical furnishings of a male Arab room.

13
Zanzibar has an ancient civilisation going
back more than a thousand years. One of
the ancient sites is Ras Mkumbuu in Pemba
where there are pillar tombs with inlaid
chinaware.

14
The old fruit market which was
located behind the Old Fort.

THE ECONOMY

15
An Arab landowner being visited by a
colonial official riding a horse.

16

Coconuts are the second major crop of Zanzibar, supplying a variety of needs of the inhabitants. This sign prohibiting trespass, in English and Arabic, lies in a coconut plantation administered by the Beit al-Mal (Administrator-General).

17

Cloves have been one of the mainstays of Zanzibar's economy. A narrow road winding through a clove plantation.

18

A typical thatched hut, with a large number of women and children involved in harvesting cloves.

19

A typical view of a settlement in the plantation
area with dense vegetation of bananas, fruit trees
and coconut palms, and a thatched hut.

20

A fishing village on the east coast of Unguja. Hanging on the wall of the house on the left is part of a fish trap. These villages were typically built in a thick grove of coconut palms. In the centre are colonial officials, including Lloyd Mathews, the First Minister appointed after Zanzibar became a British Protectorate in 1890.

SLAVERY

22
Domestic slaves chained to each other, not
showing much fear of their aged supervisor.

23

Slaves were used in the town to perform menial tasks. In this picture slaves are shown chained to a sanitation cart.

24
Girls posing for a photograph in a studio.
Note the plugs decorating their ears.

26
Slaves on the decks of a British naval ship which had rescued them, together with the captured slave traders on the left. Around 1870.

27
Slavery was abolished in Zanzibar in 1907. The Sultan's governors (Liwalis) and Muslim judges (Kadhis) are seen with British colonial officials who supervised the emancipation.

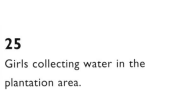

25
Girls collecting water in the plantation area.

COMMERCE

28

Dhows played a critical role in the trade of
Zanzibar, transporting goods between vari-
ous regions around the western Indian
Ocean. During the lull between the two
monsoon seasons they were careened in
the Darajani Creek.

Some of the ivory tusks were so large that they required as many as four people to carry them.

29

A major section of the merchant class were Indians. Here prominent members of the Ismaili community are seen with the Aga Khan III who visited Zanzibar in 1899 and 1905.

30

One of the major commodities of trade was ivory, transported by human porters from the interior of Africa.

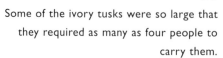

EXPLORERS & MISSIONARIES

33
St. Joseph's Roman Catholic Cathedral, built in 1896, was designed by the architect who designed the basilica of Marseilles. Among their early converts were freed slaves, here seen wearing French-type berets and Arab-type loin cloths.

32
Zanzibar was a major centre from where explorers organised their expeditions into the interior of Africa. American journalist and explorer Henry Morton Stanley met Zanzibari dignitaries during his sojourn on the island after his return from the heart of Africa in search of David Livingstone.

34

Christians were allowed to practise their religion freely in Zanzibar. The Anglicans built their cathedral on the site of the former slave market. In the foreground is the Creek at low tide.

35
An inside view of the Anglican Cathedral.

36

An English missionary lady, Miss Thackeray, with emancipated
slaves, at Mbweni, south of Zanzibar town.

THE
PALACE COMPLEX
& BOMBARDMENT OF 1896

39

The old tower which formerly stood in front
of the Beit al-Ajaib. It was demolished after
the bombardment of 1896.

38

The Palace Complex before the
Bombardment of 1896, showing the old
Beit al-Hukm in the centre, the Palace on
the left, and Beit al-Ajaib on the right. All
these buildings were connected by *wikios,*
covered passages above street level, to
permit royal ladies to move without being
seen.

41

Front view of Beit al-Ajaib and Beit
al-Hukm after the bombardment.

40

The Palace Complex after the bombardment.

42

Side view of the custums' building and Beit
al-Ajaib with the Sultans' Palace ahead
after the bombardment.

43

Destruction inside the Palace. Note the enormous chandeliers which may have been damaged but escaped total destruction.

44, 45

Side view of the Palace, with and without
the intricate wooden verandahs, destroyed
by the bombardment.

HISTORICAL ZANZIBAR

Reconstruction of Beit al-Ajaib after the Bombardment. A tower was added on its roof in place of the former separate tower which had to be demolished.

The British 'Blue Jackets' in front of Beit al Ajaib after the Bombardment.

48

Beit al-Ajaib after reconstruction. The rubble of Beit al-Hukm has been cleared to make way for a garden, and the Palace on the left has been greatly reduced in size. A temporary iron lighthouse on the right, set up after the bombardment, was later removed.

COLONIAL ZANZIBAR

50

Seyyid Hamed bin Thuwain, Ruler of Zanzibar (1893-96). On the death of the last son of Seyyid Said, the British colonial rulers chose the grandson from Oman who seemed to be most submissive to British rule.

51

Seyyid Humoud bin Muhammad, Ruler of Zanzibar (1896-1902), another grandson, who was placed on the throne after the Bombardment of 1896.

52

Real power lay in the hands of the British Resident. The Residency was designed by John Sinclair, a colonial official and architect. He designed many other buildings in Zanzibar town, including the High Court and the Peace Memorial Museum.

53

Celebration of Queen Victoria's Diamond Jubilee in 1897.

Main Road (now Kenyatta Road) decorated to welcome a distinguished visitor to 'the Emerald Island'; (left) note the rail line along the street; (right) near the Post Office.

56

Horse-drawn carriages, escorted by guards
wearing imperial Indian-type uniforms, visiting
one of the country palaces of the Sultan.

57

The Sultan's barge, presented to the Sultan
of Zanzibar by Queen Victoria.

58

The Sultan of Zanzibar, Seyyid Khalifa bin
Haroub, with colonial governors of British
East African territories.

59
The Sultan of Zanzibar, Seyyid Khalifa (holding a tennis racket), standing next to some English friends during his visit to England in 1929.

60

The Sultan of Zanzibar, Seyyid Khalifa, at a tea party with colonial and local dignitaries.

61

A colonial official with Arab dignitaries. On the far right is the famous Arab trader of the Congo, Tippu Tip.

62
Colonial officials and their wives posing
for a group photograph.

63
A colonial official on an inspection tour of the
countryside, riding a donkey, while the
local person in the middle is holding a bicycle.

64

The Zanzibar army was reorganised by
British officers in the 1880s. Zanzibar soldiers in their ceremonial uniform, with
their officers.

65

After the declaration of Zanzibar as a
Protectorate, the British established
'Her Britannic Majesty's Court' side by
side with the Muslim *Kadhis* courts.
A sitting of the Court, with Arab and
Indian interpreters.

66

A small but efficient civil service was a hallmark of a colonial regime. While retaining the top positions, the British employed Indian clerks as the middle cadre, and local people as messengers and policemen.

ECONOMIC DEVELOPMENT

68

A House near the Clove Growers
Association which has now collapsed.

69

The Bububu Railway extended for seven miles from its yard in the Old Fort to Bububu at the edge of the clove plantation area in the north. It was built by an American company in 1906, but the ubiquitous lorry buses cut short the age of the railways in Zanzibar. The rails were uprooted in 1927.

70

Railway lines passing through the Malindi quarter of Zanzibar.

71

In the 1920s the New Harbour was built
at Malindi. Rail lines were laid to
Chukwani quarries to bring stones for the
Harbour Works.

72

Chukwani, where stones for the Harbour
Works were quarried and transported on
the railway.

73

The small-gauge railway used to transport material for the Harbour Works.

74

The Harbour taking shape on the reclaimed land at Malindi.

75

View of the town from the Harbour. On
the left is the Ithna'sheri Dispensary which
formerly lay near the seashore, but the
storage *godowns* placed it in the back-
ground.

76

A horse-drawn ambulance in Zanzibar, 1904.

77

The launching of *M. V. Seyyid Khalifa,* which was built in the United Kingdom in the 1950s. It was later renamed Jamhuri after the Revolution, and was recently sold to a private entrepreneur.

CONSTITUTIONAL DEVELOPMENT

78

A meeting of the Legislative Council in the Victoria Garden Hall, with appointed Arab and Indian representatives to advise British colonial authorities.

79

The opening of the National Assembly by the last Sultan of Zanzibar, Seyyid Jamshid. On his right is the last British Resident, Sir George Mooring, and on his left the Speaker of the National Assembly and the Chief Justice. Further to the left are Abeid Amani Karume, the future President of Zanzibar, and Othman Shariff, another leader of the Afro-Shirazi Party.

Published in 1995 by HSP Publications
Head Office: 7 Highgate High Street, London N6 5JR U.K.
Zanzibar Office: P. O. Box 3181, 170 Gizenga Street

Introduction and captions by Professor Abdul Sheriff
Photographs from ©Zanzibar Archives

Picture Research Javed Jafferji
Production Editor Ashter Chomoko
Designed by Nick Ballantine Associates
Compiled by Ashter Chomoko & Javed Jafferji

ISBN 0-9521726-2-3

A CIP catalogue record for this book is available from the British
Library.

Printed by Tien Wah Press Ltd. Singapore.

ACKNOWLEDGMENTS

Hamad H Omar, Director of Zanzibar Archives, and his staff for
allowing the use of many of the photographs in this book.
Peter North for water colour illustration
Map updated from:
H.V Lanchester, Zanzibar Town 1923
Kevin Patience, The Bububu Railway

Back Page: The *Mihrab* in Kizamkazi mosque, known to have
been built in 1107 AD in the southern part of Zanzibar.